HOW TO START FREELANCING AS A BUSINESS ANALYST

A PRACTICAL GUIDE TO START AND SUCCEED AS A FREELANCE BUSINESS ANALYST

DIWAKAR KUMAR SINGH

Copyright © Diwakar Kumar Singh
All Rights Reserved.

ISBN 979-888555528-9

This book has been published with all efforts taken to make the material error-free after the consent of the author. However, the author and the publisher do not assume and hereby disclaim any liability to any party for any loss, damage, or disruption caused by errors or omissions, whether such errors or omissions result from negligence, accident, or any other cause.

While every effort has been made to avoid any mistake or omission, this publication is being sold on the condition and understanding that neither the author nor the publishers or printers would be liable in any manner to any person by reason of any mistake or omission in this publication or for any action taken or omitted to be taken or advice rendered or accepted on the basis of this work. For any defect in printing or binding the publishers will be liable only to replace the defective copy by another copy of this work then available.

This book is dedicated to all Business Analyst aspirants who is seeking to gain practical experience in business analysis.

Contents

Preface

Learning business analysis has never been a challenge and there are plenty of resources available online through which an aspirant can learn. The real challenge that most of the BA aspirants faces is the application of those theoretical knowledge.

Many BA aspirants connected with me on Linkedin and asked for projects in which they can work and gain practical exposure. So I wrote a post on Linkedin that how one can gain practical experience by doing freelancing projects.

After writing the post I started getting many queries on freelancing like how to get freelancing projects, which platform to use, how to create a good profile, what skills to mention, how to apply for projects, etc.

These queries gave me an idea to write a book and share my knowledge and experience with freelancing. Honestly speaking I had a great experience in freelancing in terms of money, knowledge, relationships that I made with my client. In this book, I will share all my experiences and tips to succeed in freelancing.

CHAPTER ONE

Why Freelancing? Benefits and Challenges

I started doing freelancing to earn some extra money. I was free on weekends so thought of utilizing the time to add extra income. I was already an experienced business analyst so my goal was not to gain practical experience however a BA aspirant can definitely do freelancing with this goal.

So here are few benefits of doing freelancing:

1. You get an opportunity to build a good relationship with client for whom you work. This can help you in getting more projects in future.

2. With a good relationship and your good work there is a chance that the freelance opportunity can turn out into a long term opportunity. By this, you dont need to look for jobs outside. I got this offer several times however I did not want to leave my company.

3. You gain that practical experience.

4. You earn money which makes you financially stable.

Here are few challenges that you can come across:

1. Finding your first project might take some time so you should not give up. You should keep on applying for projects.

2. Some projects might require prior knowledge and experience in certain domain so you have to look for projects which dont have such domain criteria.

3. Some clients may request you to show previous sample works like BRD, FRD, User stories, wireframes etc. that you have created. If you have not worked previously as a BA then it would be a challenge to show such work.

4. Sometimes it would be difficult to manage time if you are a full time employee working in any organization as you will have to manage both

your full time job and freelancing work. It will definitely test your time management skills.

Challenges will come across your way but you need to face them and move ahead.

CHAPTER TWO

Top 3 Freelancing Platform for Business Analyst

There are lot of online freelancing platforms available however my favourite top 3 platforms are:

1. Upwork: For me, Upwork has been the best freelancing platform as most of the BA projects I have got here. Irrespective of what type of freelancer you are, Upwork is one of the best platform for finding work with zero investment.

2. Freelancer: I got 2 business analysis projects projects on this platform however both were very small projects. The wide variety of specializations makes it one of the best freelancing platform. You can filter jobs by different categories like fixed price projects, hourly rate projects, contests, skills, and languages. Every job listing shows an average bid along with the current number of bidders, so you know what to expect before applying.

3. LinkedIn: I believe every professional today has a profile on LinkedIn. It is a great platform to showcase your skills, build your network and connect with clients. One of the great feature LinkedIn has is LinkedIn ProFinder, which helps businesses find freelancers who are qualified to work for them. It sends project leads to you through email, giving you the chance to write a proposal and bid. Additionally, LinkedIn job postings — helps you in finding a full-time freelance work.

CHAPTER THREE

So From Which Platform to Start With?

I would personally recommend you to start with Upwork as I had a great experience on this platform. Let me give you a brief overview of Upwork Connects:

1. After creating your profile on Upwork you receive 50-80 connects for free which you can use to bid for projects. Connects are nothing but kind of token amount which is used to place a bid on this portal. So each project requires some connects from freelancers to place a bid - 2 or 4 or 6. It will vary from project to project. You have to spend this connects very carefully. If you exhaust all your connects then you will have to purchase these connects to apply for more projects,

2. You can receive extra connects by taking Upwork Readiness Test. I received 50 connects when I cleared this test. The test is all about your knowledge of Upwork platform which is easy to clear.

3. Additionally you will receive 10 free connects every month if you have a basic account. Freelancer Plus account members receive 80 free Connects each month. I would suggest to start with a basic account only. I did all my projects with a basic account only.

4. You earn bonus 10 connects when you submit a proposal to a client and win an interview.

To summarize, I can say that you can start your freelancing on upwork with a maximum of 130 connects which means you can apply to a maximum of 24 projects in the first month.

I applied to 9 projects on the first day out of which I got revert from 2 clients and later got both the projects. So without spending a penny I earned two projects. Isn't it interesting?

CHAPTER FOUR

Creating Profile on Upwork

Now you have understood about connects and its importance, lets understand how to create a good profile on Upwork. I will discuss all the steps and attach screenshots to explain wherever required.

Firstly you will have to search Upwork on Google and complete the sign up process. I will not discuss the sign up process as that is a very straightforward step.

Once you have completed the sign up process you will be redirected to a page where you need to answer three questions like have you freelanced before, your biggest goal for freelancing, and how would you like to work(I would suggest to select the first option in this)? Now click on create a profile.

The profile on Upwork can be created in 3 ways:

a) You can import your profile from Linkedin

b) By uploading your resume

c) Filling all the details manually

You can use the first or second option if your linkedin profile is updated or you have already created a good resume with all the skill sets, tools, and techniques properly highlighted.

I created the profile by manually filling all the details and will share the same with you. So lets start filling the details manually.

1. You need to add a title which will be visible to clients. I have kept as "Business Analyst".

2. You need to now add all your experience. Adding experiences increases your chance of getting projects as client can see your previous experience. Even if you have not worked as a Business Analyst before you should keep your title as a Business Analyst only and add the experience accordingly. If you are a beginner, you can add your internship experience or any projects that you did in college.

3. You then need to add your education details.

4. The next step is to add your language details.

5. Then you need to add the skills. This is a very important section as depending upon the skills you enter, upwork will recommend specific job posts to you. You can add maximum 15 skills. Here are the skills which I will recommend you to mention - Business Analysis, Requirement Analysis, Requirement Management, UML, Process Flow Diagram, Business Process Modelling, Gap Analysis, Root Cause Analysis, Stakeholder Management, Requirement Elicitation, BPMN, Jira, Atlassian Confluence, Microsoft Visio, SQL

6. The next step would be to add your Bio. Here is a sample Bio for your reference.

" I am an experienced(or you can say certified) business analyst with X years of experience in _____________ domain supporting business solution software and analyzing business operations. If you are looking for a business analyst in your project- I can help!

1. I have proven experience in requirement gathering using Interviews, workshops, Focused groups, brainstorming and prototyping techniques.

2. I have extensive experience in business documentation(BRD,FRD,SRS and Use cases), business process flow mapping(BPMN2.0, UML, Use Case Diagram), and business process improvement

3. Experienced in system gap analysis (AS-IS and To-Be), PARETO analysis, SWOT analysis, root cause analysis(using 5 Why and 7 So What technique).

4. I have proven experience in system enhancements, designing, development, testing and maintenance of applications.

5. Experienced in Prioritizing requirements using strong prioritization skills like MOSCOW, 100 Dollar Method and Planning Poker.

6. I have good amount of experience in IT Services, Business Analysis, data analysis, requirement gathering, requirement analysis, design thinking, system thinking, and critical thinking.

7. I have extensive experience in using tools like Jira and Confluence for creating product backlogs, epics, user story, logging defects and requirement management.

7. I have good knowledge of modelling tools like MS Visio and Draw.io.

8. I have good knowledge of data visualization and analytics tool like Tableau, Power Bi and SQL. "

7. Now, you have to choose the categories that best describe the type of work you do. You can choose the category as Web, Mobile & Software Dev and sub category as product management. Dont worry, I understand there is no option to choose Business Analyst but this does not matter.

8. The next step is to add your hourly rate. My suggesion would be to start with a low hourly rate when you are a beginner on Upwork. According to my experience client mostly prefer BAs with hourly rate between 8-10 $.

9. The last step would be to add a professional photo and your address.

Great, you have now created your profile on Upwork and have received free connects.

CHAPTER FIVE

Its Time to Search For Projects

It is now time to look for projects. You can click on "Find Work" menu button and you will land to below screen:

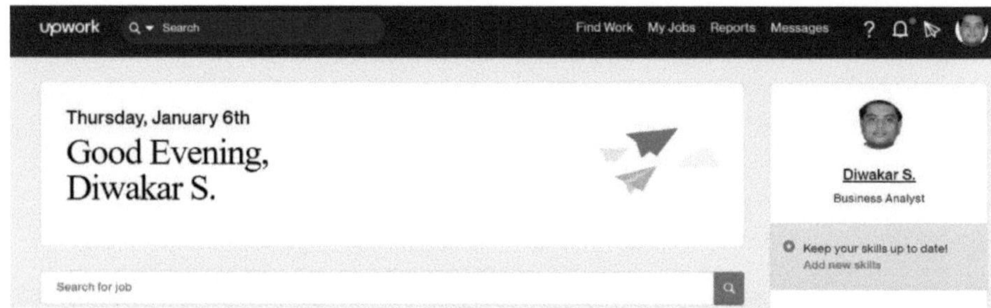

In the search bar type "Business Analyst" and search. So here is the first business analyst project that is displayed. There is also an option to sort projects which I keep as Newest so that the latest BA projects are displayed.

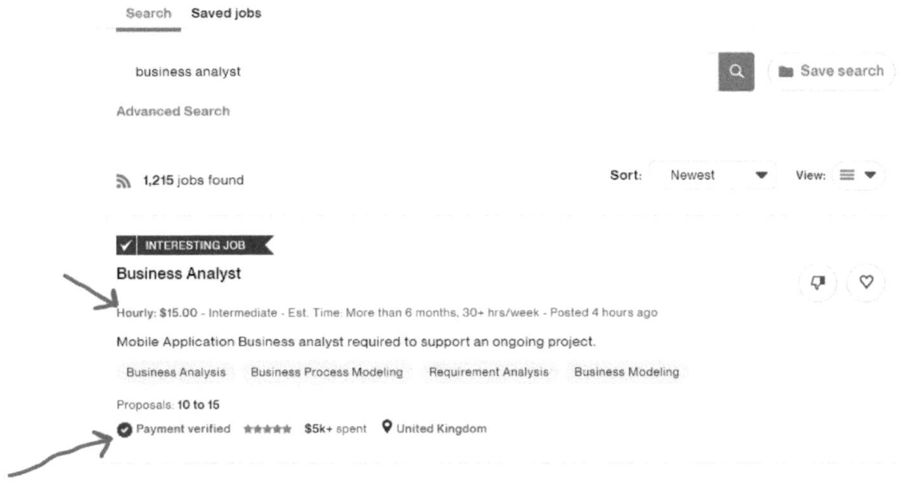

Few points to keep in mind before applying for a project.

1. Payment Method: Always check whether the payment method is verified or not. In above image you can see that the payment method is verified. If the payment method is not verified, you should not apply for those projects. For an example in below project you should not apply. There might be a possibility that the project is not that genuine so its not a good idea to waste your connects on such projects. Again, I may not be completely correct but this is just a suggestion.

2. Budget: The second thing that you should check is the budget. Ensure that the budget with which you are bidding should not exceed that and should always remain under clients budget. In the below image client has kept hourly rate as $15 so your hourly rate should not be more than this.

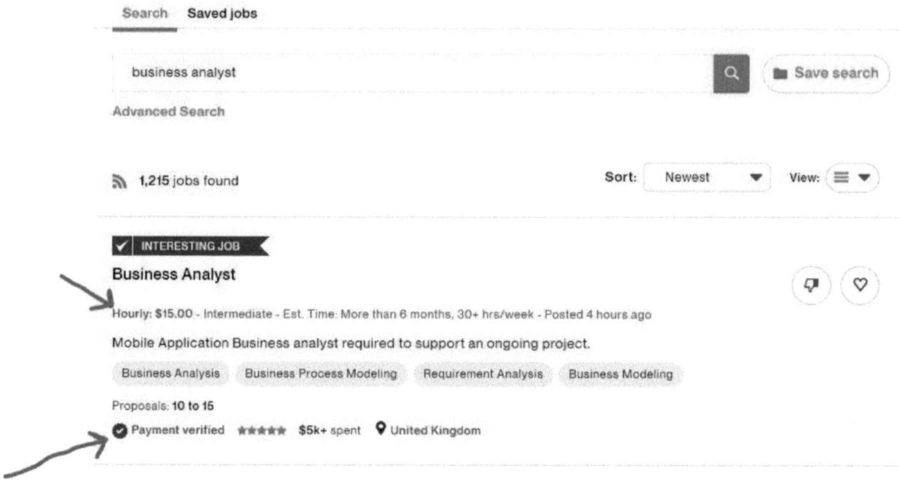

3. Job Description: Read the job description thoroughly from top to bottom. Do not rush and bid for projects. Some projects will have a lengthy descriptions but make sure you read it thoroughly to understand what is the project about and what is expected by client from you.

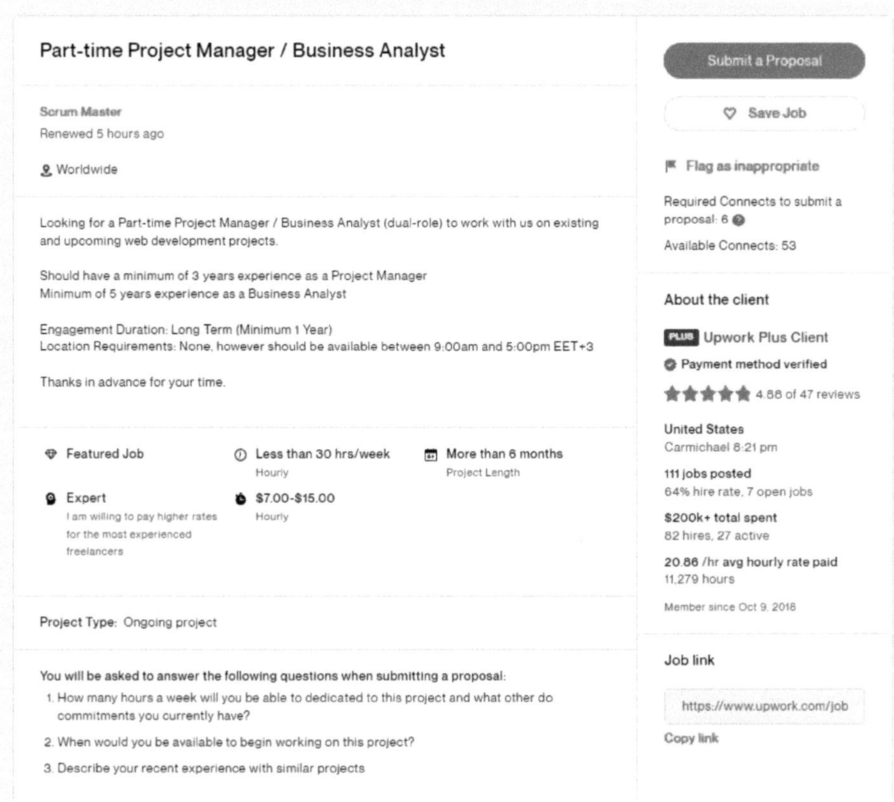

4. Checking the Connects required to apply for project: Always check whether you have required amount of connects to apply for the project or not.

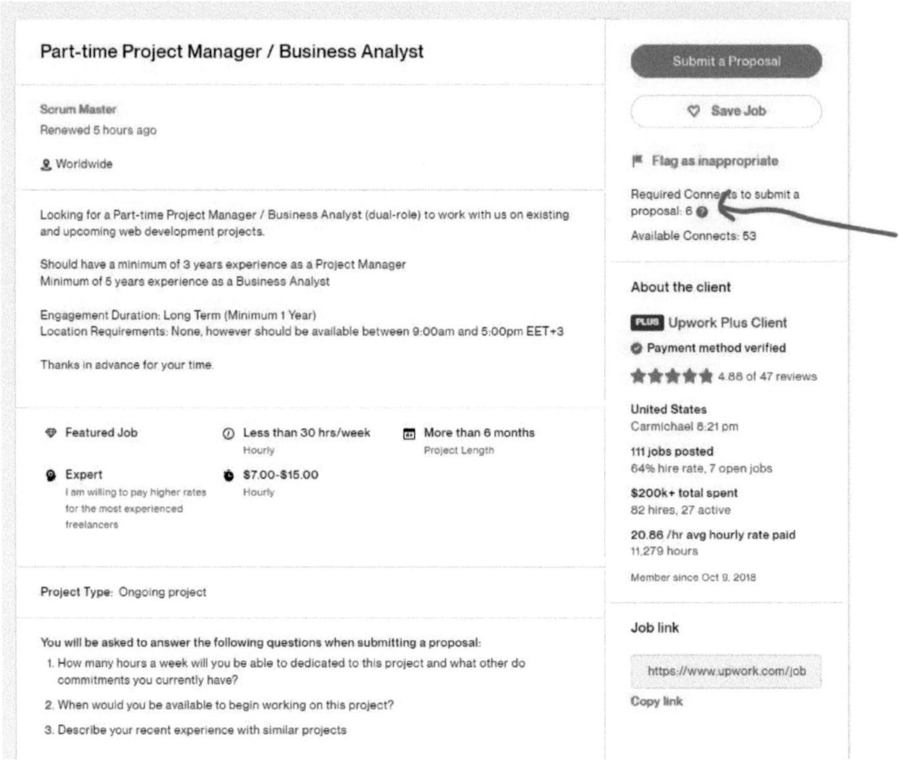

Part-time Project Manager / Business Analyst
Scrum Master
Renewed 5 hours ago
Worldwide
Looking for a Part-time Project Manager / Business Analyst (dual-role) to work with us on existing and upcoming web development projects.
Should have a minimum of 3 years experience as a Project Manager
Minimum of 5 years experience as a Business Analyst
Engagement Duration: Long Term (Minimum 1 Year)
Location Requirements: None, however should be available between 9:00am and 5:00pm EET+3
Thanks in advance for your time.
Featured Job
Less than 30 hrs/week
Hourly
More than 6 months
Project Length
Expert
I am willing to pay higher rates for the most experienced freelancers
$7.00-$15.00
Hourly
Project Type: Ongoing project
You will be asked to answer the following questions when submitting a proposal:
1. How many hours a week will you be able to dedicated to this project and what other do commitments you currently have?
2. When would you be available to begin working on this project?
3. Describe your recent experience with similar projects
Submit a Proposal
Save Job
Flag as inappropriate
Required Connects to submit a proposal: 6
Available Connects: 53
About the client
PLUS Upwork Plus Client
Payment method verified
4.88 of 47 reviews
United States
Carmichael 8:21 pm
111 jobs posted
64% hire rate, 7 open jobs
$200k+ total spent
82 hires, 27 active
20.86 /hr avg hourly rate paid
11,279 hours
Member since Oct 9, 2018
Job link
https://www.upwork.com/job
Copy link

5. Checking total number of proposals for the project: In the below image, there has been 10 to 15 proposals already been made bu freelancers so the chances are less that you get shortlisted for this project so its not a good idea to spend your connects on such projects.

Business Analyst
Hourly: $15.00-$25.00 - Intermediate - Est. Time: More than 6 months, 30+ hrs/week - Posted 5 hours ago
Summary Acts as a liaison among stakeholders, process owners, and IT to provide strategic guidance for initiatives that enable the organization to achieve its goals. Includes independently working side-by-side with business process owners and key sta ... more
Business Analysis
Proposals: 10 to 15
PLUS Payment verified $600k+ spent Ireland

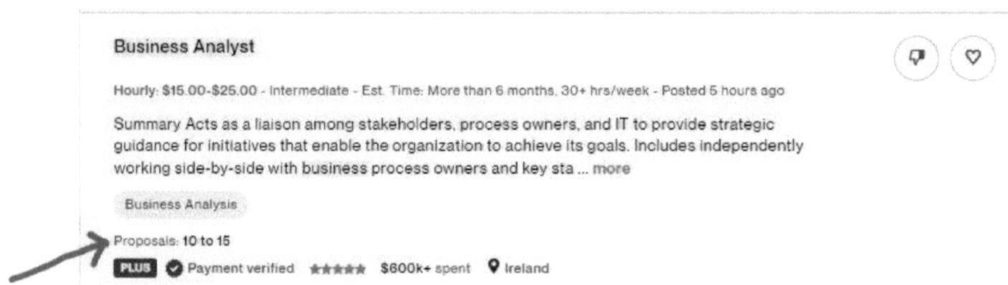

Whereas in below project the number of proposals made is less than 5 so your chances are high here.

6. Checking Skills and Expertise mentioned for the project: Always check the mentioned skills mentioned in the project, if you think that your skillsets are not matching then do not apply to those projects.

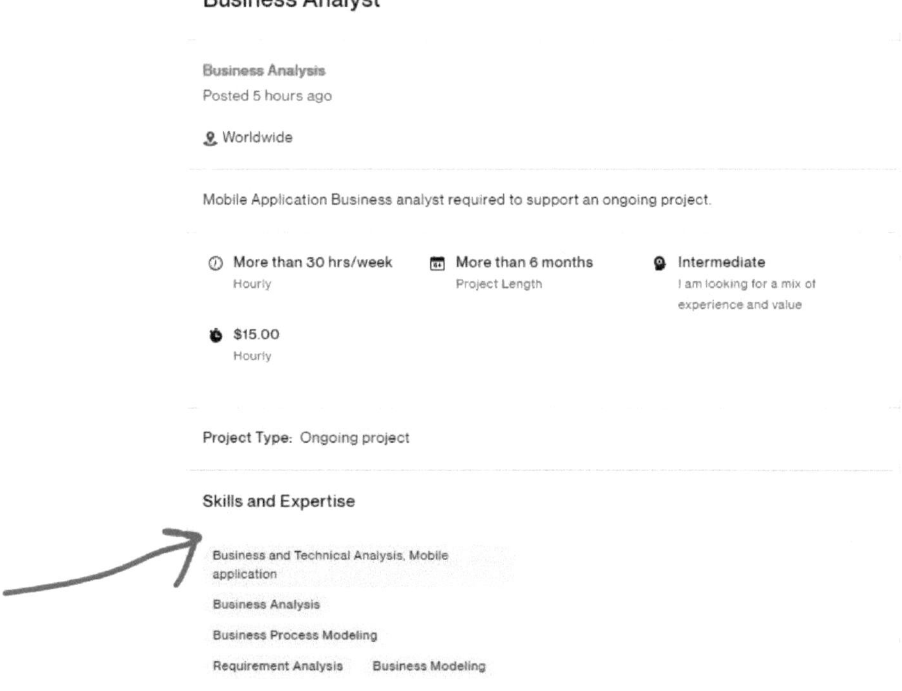

7. Checking Preferred Qualifications posted by Client: In some projects you will see client has posted some additional criteria under "Preferred Qualifications". If you meet all the preferred Qualification criteria you will see a red tick as shown in the image. You should not apply to projects where you dont have a green tick.

Avoid applying to below project as it has only one green tick. This is visible to client when you submit a proposal which indicates you do not meet all the criterias.

8. Additional questions: In some projects client will post additional questions which you must answer before submitting a proposal. Remember if you dont answer all the questions it is very likely that your proposal will be rejected by client.

You will be asked to answer the following questions when submitting a proposal:

1. Do you have any experience working with Power BI?
2. Please describe your level of expertise with Tableau
3. Do you have a link to your dashboards portfolio? Please share it with us
4. Please list any certifications related to this project

CHAPTER SIX

Submitting a Proposal

Now that you are aware of all the pointers and you have decided to bid for a project, here are the some useful tips that will help you in submitting a proposal.

I will share a sample project in which I placed a bid and I got that project. So, below is the job description of one of the projects in which I placed a bid and won the project.

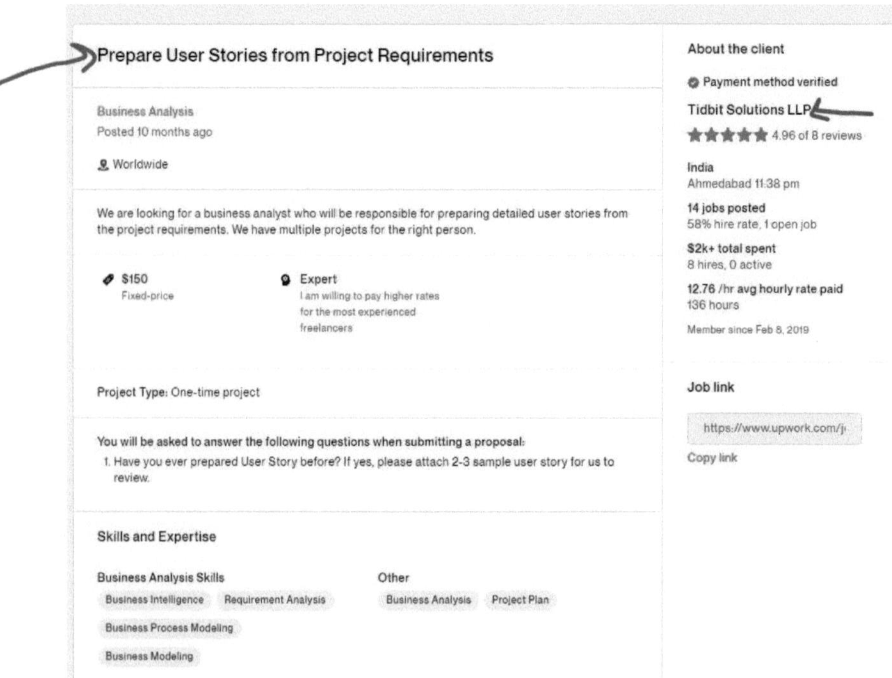

Here is my cover letter for this job: Firstly I read the job description and picked up the keywords mentioned in it which was **user story** and ensured to include it in my cover letter.

Note:- Never apply to all jobs with the same cover letter. Read the job description thoroughly, pick up the keywords and mention it in your cover letter.

Cover letter

Dear Hiring Manager,

Hope you are doing good in this pandemic.

I am writing this letter to express my keen interest in working as a Business Analyst for this project

I am detail-oriented technocrat with over 5 years of experience in IT, Insurance, Ecommerce, Travel and HRMS(HR and Payroll system) domain supporting business solution software and analyzing business operations. I have proven experience in requirement gathering, project management, business process flow mapping(BPMN2.0, UML, Use Cases), business analysis & business process improvement, system gap analysis (AS-IS and To-Be) and enhancements, designing, development, testing and maintenance of client applications by utilizing strong prioritization skills(MOSCOW) and analytical ability to achieve the goal.

I have good amount of experience in IT Services, Business Analysis, data analysis, requirement gathering, requirement analysis, design thinking, system thinking, critical thinking, functional testing, UAT and client management. I am adept at tools such as Jira and Confluence which is being used to create product backlogs, Sepics, epics, user story, logging defects and ensuring deliver of product as per agile framework.

I also possess strong interpersonal skills that help in effectively interacting with the customers, business consultants, subject matter experts and product development team to provide the ultimate solution for clients over major market like US, APAC, Europe, LATAM and MEA. Hence, I am eager to put my skills to work in a capacity that will allow me the opportunity to further my professional development.

As we all know that COVID-19 pandemic has paved the way for a paradigm shift, it permits the workforce to have access remotely across the globe. In the said context, I would like to ensure that I am available to work remotely and I have been delivering equally efficient results in my current work from home profile in terms of customer support and project management.

My resume is enclosed for your consideration. I look forward to hearing from you soon.

I appreciate your time and consideration.

Sincerely,

Diwakar Kumar Singh less

Here is the response from client:

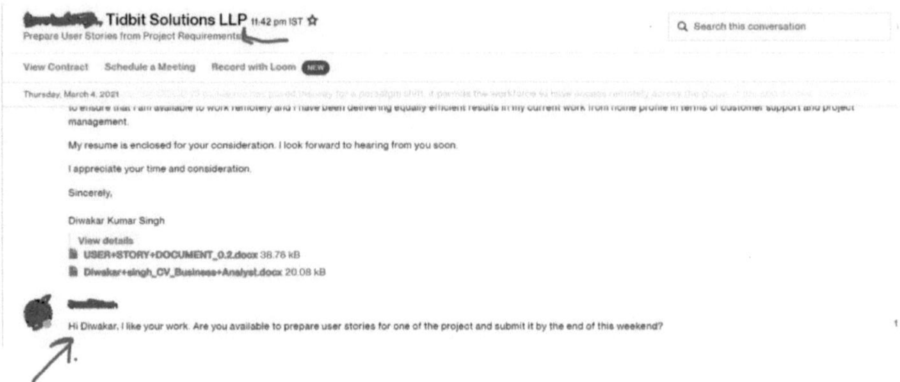

Here is what I earnt from this project:

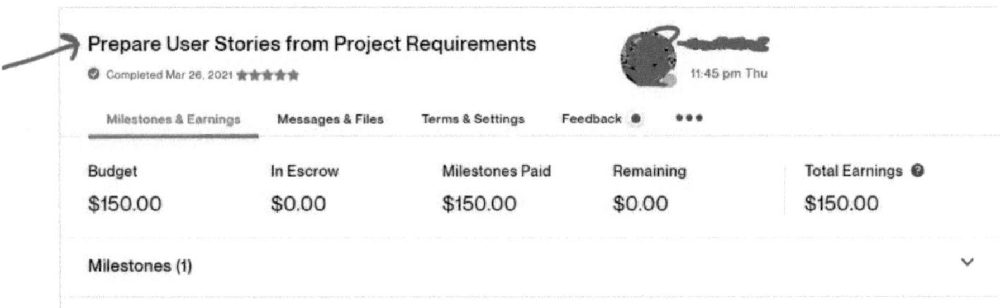

So this project did not required any domain knowledge, any prior BA experience. I got this project only on the basis of a sample user story document that I submitted. Client liked my sample document and I got the project.

It was a great learning experience from the project as the work was not only to write user stories but also to elicit requirement from customer who was based in UK.

Conclusion

There are lot of opportunities on Upwork for business analysis work. You need to invest time and look for the right project matching your skillsets. You may not get your first project after couple of bids and may take time but you have to keep on looking for projects.

Believe me you will soon get a project where you can work, gain the practical experience, learn, and earn money. I had invested a lot of time in writing this book and hope that it helps you in some way. Do let me know your feedback by emailing me at **info.bahelpline@gmail.com**

Printed by Libri Plureos GmbH in Hamburg,
Germany